I'm Leaving...

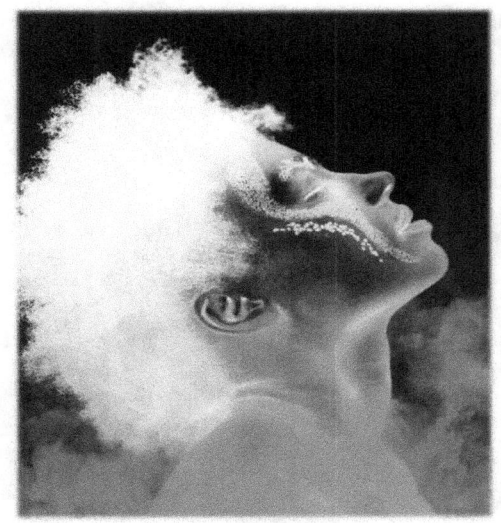

Postdated Goodbyes

L. TERRELL

Copyright © 2019 by LaToya C. Terrell
All rights reserved.
Front Cover Image by Kaci Jade Carson
Book Design by LaToya Terrell
Printed in the United States of America
First Printing Edition, 2019
ISBN: 9781671192164

*To any and every one that is or has been Saudade…
this one's for you.*

CONTENTS

Homesick   1

Mundane Life   5

Goodbye   9

Content   13

Already Gone   16

Thank You   21

Table of Contents

HOMESICK

I USE TO BELIEVE "HOME" WAS A PLACE

THE PHYSICAL COUNTRY YOU'RE BORN

A BUILDING STRUCTURE IN WHICH YOU RESIDE

SOMEWHERE IN THIS WORLD YOU COULD RUN TO

A SAFE PLACE TO HIDE

I OFTEN WONDER WHAT IT'D BE LIKE...

TO TRULY HAVE "HOME"

WHEN AND WHERE WOULD I DISCOVER IT?

REALIZING "HOME" IS NOT SIMPLY A TANGIBLE PLACE

IT'S A FEELING TOO

HOME IS PALPABLE

IT IS YOU...

A FUTURE "HOME" I'M MAKING PREPARATIONS TO MOVE INTO

WHERE FAMILIARITY IS AND PRIDE CAN'T RESIST

NO MATTER HOW HARD I TRY, I FIND THAT TOO...

Homesick

"Home" is me--or rather "her"

A distant self that I miss.

I miss myself

It's her I miss?

That I long for?

Not only that, a desire so true I'm having is her with you?

Still I wonder what it'd be like...

To truly have "home"

In leaving I know that I'll soon reunite her,

That part of me I unknowingly pushed away,

She got left behind and now I find myself...

Homesick.

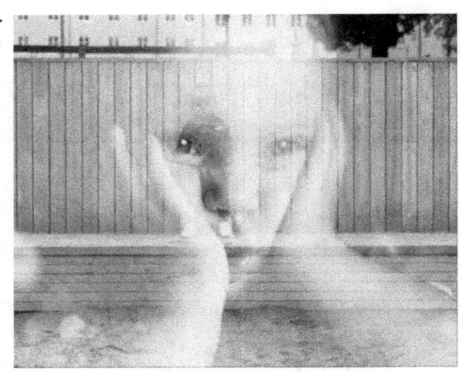

Photo credit:@jens_johnsson

Mundane Life

It's troubling, knowing…
I shouldn't complain
But it's a bit too unsettling…
Stagnant life.
*Questioning "**Am I'm settling?**"*
Hiding inside…

Hard to breath masquerading
Within a shell of past-self trying to revive
who's already died.
Attempting well living in her normality,
When she's dead and now I'm dying!
Can't breathe…
While trying
to resume indefinitely in her place.

There was a time I cried and pleaded with God
for this life…
To be in this place. "If I could just finish it and achieve that"; I'd say…
It was another time.
Before I-had a taste of true self and her life.
He wouldn't give it
Know I understand why

TORN WHEN HERE IS WHERE I WANT TO TRY AND BE "OKAY" FOR REASONS I CAN'T SAY...
YET I KNOW I CAN'T STAY.
MISPLACED GUILT OF NOT WANTING TO WANT TO GO...
IT CAN'T BE HELPED I WANT TO GO.
HAUNTED BY THIS GLIMPSE OF FUTURE LIFE, I CAN'T LET GO. I CAN NO LONGER HIDE, AND MUST RESUME BEYOND THE...

MUNDANE LIFE.

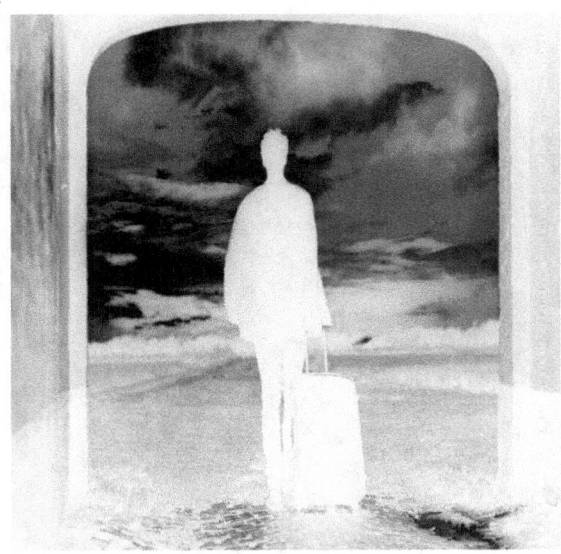

Mundane Life

Photo credit: by Mantas Hesthaven

GOODBYE

Why?
----X

It's hard to explain, yet I'll try--to express the "Why" behind this "Goodbye". A Goodbye that will cause some to cry and others to never bat an eye-won't last much longer here. Some know and others don't.

A time before I had to go. Which open doors inside my soul that lead to places even I didn't know; existed...within it. Narrow tunnels, loose gravel, dark roads mountains upon mountains of the unknown.

I had to go...need to go.

She was here, then went to return again...scratch that. Not "I", but *her*, who was me from before...who is back-not again, yet I came here. While I'm here don't...only miss me when I'm gone.

Her, this me, initially was never here before; birth elsewhere-from elsewhere I was there. A witness-this is... hard to explain.

Not simple to say.
----X

I was born in the sky, and *her*? There she died. I tried; Lord knows my efforts and my might. Worked hard to hardly working; this isn't working...Suddenly, or just may be...could be; it's been like this and I chose to ignore it. Or for a while found comfort in the simple bliss? Oblivious to the truth of knowing I don't fit where *she* originally did. I'm going.

Created to fly, born in the sky.

- - - - - ✕

Bittersweet knowing, only...leaving will cure me.

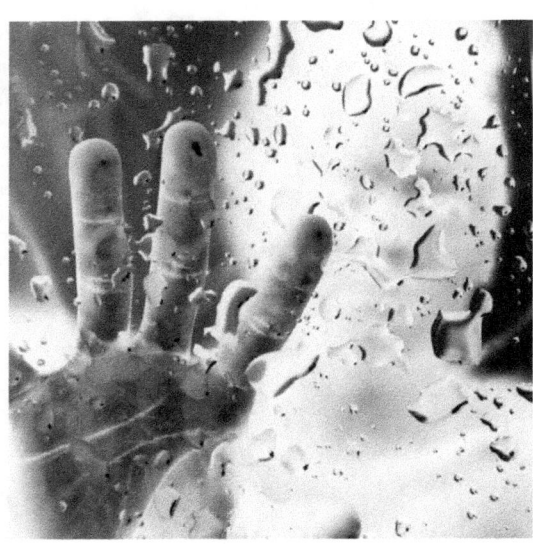

Assuring soul screaming *"Let go...just go!"* Stagnant life--tears in each eye...before I die ***I'm going.***

Goodbye.

Photo credit: @kaci_caleb3.

CONTENT

I was content with self before you gave word of

something else.

Why tell me now? Nudging my attention towards

him and even go as far as giving vivid details about

a soul destined-yet-YOU don't send?

As for me...

I was content with self before you gave word of

something else.

Now knowing abruptly, haunts me daily in the mist

of quiet moments of solitude I find myself

wondering when will You finally allow ***him*** and I to

become we; into one?

Because...

I was content with self before you gave word of

something else.

Inducing eruption through my world...

causing life changing pounder as I pray in wonder.

Your words *only* I live to die for.

In spite of...

I was content with self before you gave word of

something else...

Wasn't I*?*

Content.

(© La Toya Terrell 2017)

Already Gone

I had to learn how strong I truly am.

I had to learn that I am bolder than I ever thought myself to be.

I had to learn that I have heart for all that I've anxiously stated I'd never do, avoided or even hated...

I had to learn that, to you folks will do the extent of measures you allow them to.

I had to learn how to speak up not just when spoken to...and how not to settle into a role I've remold myself to fit into. With that said, I had to learn the warning signs behind a season nearing its end and begin to learn when to say when and even then...

I had to learn it again, that fitting a need not permanently meant for me is usually doing a thing I'm extremely good at yet by no means should necessarily be doing that.

I had to learn that once I left I had already reached a point of no return...upon return it wasn't me...

Already Gone

Already Gone.

Photo credit: @blakeguidry

Thank You

Rather constructively stating or bitterly hating...
Thanks for mentioning that.

I get it; you invested your time listening to a speech
she spoke a song he performed or was it something
I wrote?
Ah yes, thanks for mentioning that.
These thoughts that I've written
definitely could have used a critic or salty cynic
who couldn't give two cents towards another soul's
sentiments...
still, thanks for mentioning that.

Now let's put it to a vote...that speech she spoke,
song he performed or thing I wrote...
Was it meant *specifically* for you?
Right...
Allow me to say, our mistake in underestimating
your capability of intellectually determining that the
portions of ourselves we chose to share with the
world is for or simply not meant to resonate with you. With that said, rather constructively stating or bitterly hating... Thanks for mentioning that.

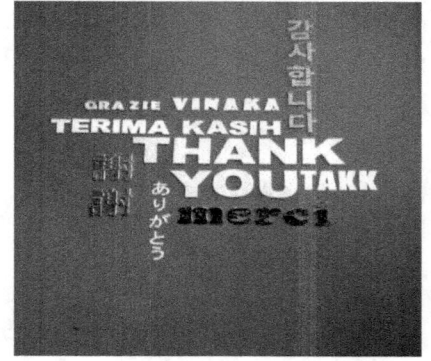

©LaToya Terrell 2019
Photo credit: @liplip

Souloetic Thoughts Series, Book I

I'm Leaving...
Postdated Goodbyes

www.ingramcontent.com/pod-product-compliance
Lightning Source LLC
Chambersburg PA
CBHW072026230526
45466CB00019B/901